Richard Matthews
Welfare Island
New York City

𝕿𝖍𝖊 𝕮𝖆𝖒𝖇𝖗𝖎𝖉𝖌𝖊 𝕻𝖔𝖊𝖙𝖘

General Editor, BLISS PERRY

Edited by

BROWNING	HORACE E. SCUDDER
MRS. BROWNING	HARRIET WATERS PRESTON
BURNS	W. E. HENLEY
BYRON	PAUL E. MORE
DRYDEN	GEORGE R. NOYES
ENGLISH AND SCOTTISH }	HELEN CHILD SARGENT
POPULAR BALLADS	GEORGE L. KITTREDGE
HOLMES	HORACE E. SCUDDER
KEATS	HORACE E. SCUDDER
LONGFELLOW	HORACE E. SCUDDER
LOWELL	HORACE E. SCUDDER
MILTON	WILLIAM VAUGHN MOODY
POPE	HENRY W. BOYNTON
SCOTT	HORACE E. SCUDDER
SHAKESPEARE	W. A. NEILSON
SHELLEY	GEORGE E. WOODBERRY
SPENSER	R. E. NEIL DODGE
TENNYSON	WILLIAM J. ROLFE
WHITTIER	HORACE E. SCUDDER
WORDSWORTH	A. J. GEORGE

In Preparation

CHAUCER	F. N. ROBINSON

HOUGHTON MIFFLIN COMPANY

BOSTON AND NEW YORK

The Cambridge Edition of the Poets

EDITED BY

HORACE E. SCUDDER

SCOTT

BY THE EDITOR

THE
COMPLETE POETICAL WORKS OF
SIR WALTER SCOTT

Cambridge Edition

BOSTON AND NEW YORK
HOUGHTON MIFFLIN COMPANY
The Riverside Press Cambridge

THE
COMPLETE POETICAL WORKS OF
SIR WALTER SCOTT
Cambridge Edition

Ashestiel

BOSTON AND NEW YORK
HOUGHTON MIFFLIN COMPANY
The Riverside Press, Cambridge

EDITOR'S NOTE

WHEN Dr. Rolfe edited *The Poetical Works of Sir Walter Scott, Baronet,* in 1887, he made a critical examination of the several texts, with the result of discovering many errors and inconsistencies in the current editions. The text which he thus established may be regarded as accurate and trustworthy. It has been adopted, so far as it goes, in the present *Cambridge Edition.* Dr. Rolfe, however, was preparing a volume which, by calling in the aid of new and faithful illustrations, should appeal through its beauty and choiceness to lovers of Scott who might be supposed to know their author and to desire a fit and convenient edition of his poems. He excluded purposely a number of less important poems, and grouped all the minor poems in sections following the series of long narrative poems. At the close he added a body of notes and prefaces, drawn from Scott's own editions.

In accordance with the general plan of the *Cambridge* series, the present editor has undertaken to give the entire body of Sir Walter's poetry and to arrange it with as close an approach to strict chronological order as was possible without pedantry. He has prefaced each poem or group of poems with notes describing the origin or circumstance of composition, and in these notes has included Scott's own Introductions, and such references as occur in Lockhart, in Scott's *Letters,* and in his *Journal.* In this way he has undertaken to separate the history of a poem from the explication of its parts.

For the latter, he has had recourse for the most part in the *Notes and Illustrations* to the notes written and gathered by Scott for his collective edition. Scott's unfailing interest in everything Scottish led him to great lengths in his annotation and especially to the accumulation of a great deal of antiquarian and sometimes rather remote material. He forgot his poem and even now and then apparently the subject itself as he heaped up illustrations. The editor therefore has found it expedient, while retaining Scott's own notes, to omit some of the discursive portions drawn from other writers. The annotation, moreover, is made in one respect more convenient and compact by the explanation of rare and local words in a *Glossary* which is an enlargement of the one accompanying Dr. Rolfe's volume.

In his *Biographical Sketch,* the Editor has had in view more especially that portion of Scott's life which closed with the great poetical period, since it is Scott the poet who is especially under consideration. He was glad to avail himself of the admirable and suggestive interpretation of the poet's life made by Ruskin in *Fors Clavigera.*

CAMBRIDGE, March, 1900.

TABLE OF CONTENTS